Oct. 201

D0290716

I love you, Phyx!
Hopefully, this will
make you laugh
about the cat. :)

Liz

Other 'crazy' gigglebooks by Bill Stott

Sex – it drives us crazy!
Marriage – it drives us crazy!
Football – it drives us crazy!
Rugby – it drives us crazy!

Published simultaneously in 2004 by Exley Publications Ltd in Great Britain, and Exley Publications LLC in the USA

12 11 10 9 8 7 6 5 4 3 2

Selection and arrangement copyright © 2004 Helen Exley
Cartoons copyright © 2004 Bill Stott
Design by 451° <studio@451.uk.com>

ISBN 1-86187-754-4

A copy of the CIP data is available from the British Library on request.
All rights reserved. No part of this publication may be reproduced or transmitted in any form or by any means without permission in writing from the publisher.

Printed in China

Helen Exley Giftbooks, 16 Chalk Hill, Watford, Herts, WD19 4BG, UK
Helen Exley Giftbooks, 185 Main Street, Spencer MA 01562, USA
www.helenexleygiftbooks.com

A HELEN EXLEY GIGGLEBOOK

Cats

THEY DRIVE US CRAZY!

CARTOONS BY BILL STOTT

"I think that hairdryer
is too powerful for him..."

"A whole 25lb turkey? Nonsense.
No cat could eat a whole 25lb turkey."

VETINARY
SURGEON

"Don't be alarmed. It's just his way of saying 'please don't hurt me.'"

"Come on –
Dinner!"
I ate two
birds already...

"All that stuff about bringing them gifts – it's rubbish. We do it just to scare them!"

"Oh, come, come – does she look like a cat who'd make a smell?"

"O.K. a brief explanation will do.
Why is my chicken leg
in your mouth?"

"You're sitting in his chair..."

"You must tell me if he's being a nuisance..."

"There are some very distant relatives of yours on..."

WILD
CATS
OF THE
SERENGETI

"How come I get thrown out when the flea was found on the carpet?"

"Well, of course she's growling.
You put ketchup on your steak,
and she hates ketchup!"

You might think it's only a stupid leaf. But to me...

But to me it's a wildebeest on the high veld...

"Now, that's what
I call a catflap."

"Since she stayed at the Hilton,
she's become so fastidious..."

"And now –
a can opener the
cat can use!"

"And when she actually
deigns to come home,
we'll do our tiger ambush!"

YWROWWR
ROWL
ERRRR!

It's as I suspected – the oaf doesn't speak Felinese!

"Uh-oh – he knows it's cheap soya substitute."

Right first time!
KITTY

"You can tell he's a pedigree. He's the only member of the family who likes politics."

"Play with the yarn. Don't kill it!"

"They do say
that cats know
what you're
thinking."

God, I hate cats...
I'm not wild about you either, mate...

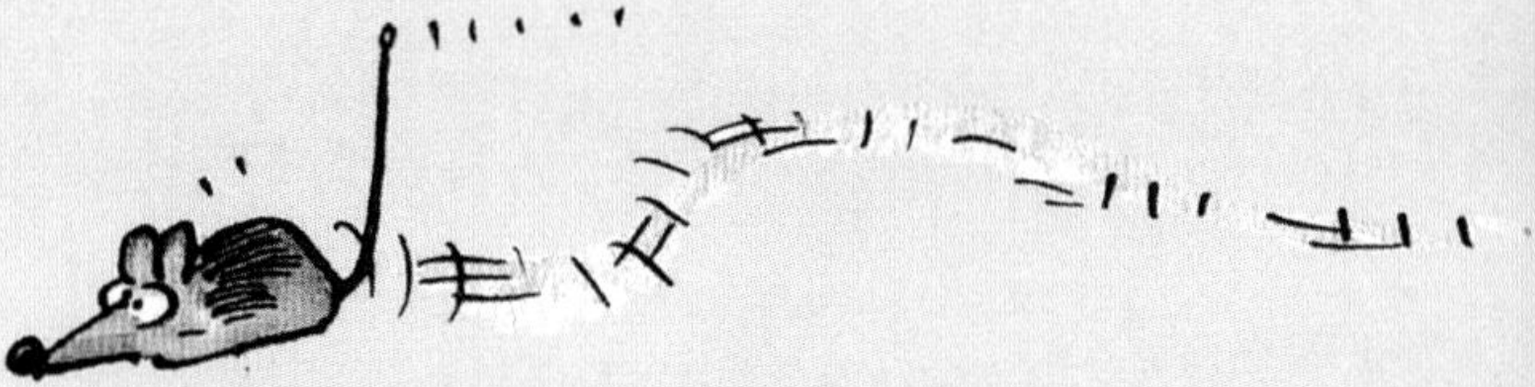

"Normally I'd have to admit you're a pretty humdrum kind of guy. But with that can-opener in your hand, you're a giant."

"Dad! Oscar doesn't seem too keen on 'Kittichews'."

PLEASE RAKE AFTER
USE Thank YOU
THE MANAGEMENT

"Here Smelly, Smelly. Here Smelly..."
PLEASE DO NOT BE OFFENDED I AM CALLING THE CAT

"Come on Rambo! Dinsie Winsies!"

"Look at me!
I love you!
I love you!
Feed me!"
What a
creep...

"Learning to climb trees is cheating!"

I know, I know, it's a scratch post – I still prefer the wallpaper...

"Harold!
Quick!
The screens!."

"What's wrong? He always washes that way – don't they all?"

KEEP YOUR
CAT OUT OF
MY VEGETABLE
PATCH!

"The twins tried out your home perm kit on Chester!"

"How many times do I have to tell you? Never change channels without asking – it's very rude..."

"Hello!
Is Tweety Face
pleased to
see me?"

"So much for your independence act!"

"What did the nasty man do to Mama's little soldier?"

SURGERY

"Louie, I'd better hang up. They're staring at me the way they always do when I use the 'phone..."

"Satisfy my curiosity – if you could get at me, would you actually eat me?"

"A simple 'yes' or 'no' will do."

"How'd you like it if I came and lay on your chest first thing in the morning?"

"I'll wait until someone comes by before I go and have a drink. I just love those cries of middle-class outrage."

"Either you come in right now, or you're out all night!"

About Bill Stott

Bill Stott is a freelance cartoonist whose work never fails to pinpoint the absurd and simply daft moments in our daily lives. Originally Head of Arts faculty at a city high school, Bill launched himself as a freelance cartoonist in 1976. With sales of 2.8 million books with Helen Exley Giftbooks, Bill has an impressive portfolio of 26 published titles, including his very successful *Spread of Over 40's Jokes* and *Triumph of Over 50's Jokes*.

Bill's work appears in many publications and magazines, ranging from the *The Times Educational Supplement* to *Practical Poultry*. An acclaimed after-dinner speaker, Bill subjects his audience to a generous helping of his wit and wisdom, illustrated with cartoons drawn deftly on the spot!

What is a Helen Exley giftbook?

We hope you enjoy *Cats – they drive us crazy!*. It's just one of many hilarious cartoon books available from Helen Exley Giftbooks, all of which make special gifts. We try our best to bring you the funniest jokes because we want every book we publish to be great to give, great to receive.

HELEN EXLEY GIFTBOOKS creates gifts for all special occasions – not just birthdays, anniversaries, weddings and Christmas, but for those times when you just want to say 'thanks' or 'I love you'. Why not visit our website, www. helenexleygiftbooks.com, and browse through all our present ideas?

ALSO BY BILL STOTT

Marriage – it drives us crazy!
Football – it drives us crazy!
Rugby – it drives us crazy!
Sex – it drives us crazy!

Information on all our titles is also available from
Helen Exley Giftbooks, 16 Chalk Hill, Watford WD19 4BG, UK. Tel 01923 250505
Helen Exley Giftbooks, 185 Main Street, Spencer MA 01562, USA. Tel 877 395 3942